How to Create Language Experts With
Literary Terms

Codi Hrouda and Emma McInerney
with Lyle Lee Jenkins

My Book of Evidence for Lessons Learned

By:

School:

Teacher:

Date:

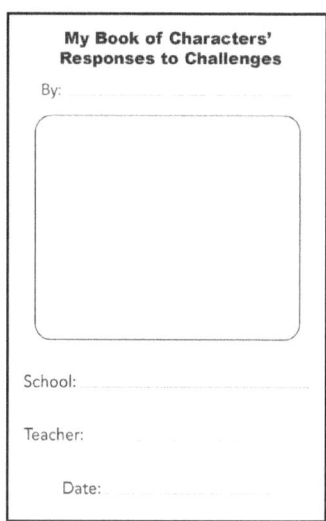

My Book of Characters' Responses to Challenges

By:

School:

Teacher:

Date:

My Book of Character's Perspectives

By:

School:

Teacher:

Date:

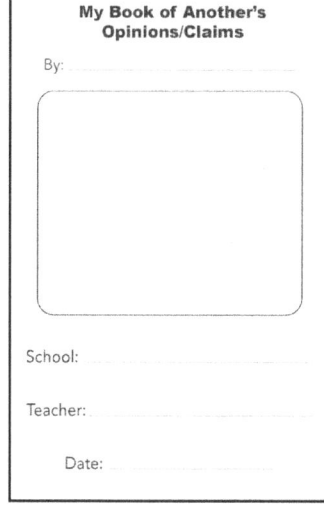

My Book of Another's Opinions/Claims

By:

School:

Teacher:

Date:

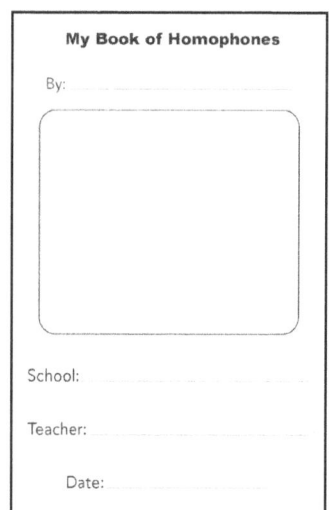

My Book of Homophones

By:

School:

Teacher:

Date:

Perfect School Collection™

To contact the authors regarding keynotes, workshops or bulk orders, visit LtoJ.net/Contact

ISBN: 978-1-956457-68-1

Book Design & Graphics: Christy Courtright, Christy's Customs LLC
Quality Assurance Manager: Kelly Lippert
Publishing Consultant: Martha Bullen, Bullen Publishing Services
Distribution Coordinator: Maggie McLaughlin

Printed in the United States of America

The Perfect School Collection™

How to Create a Perfect School by Lyle Lee Jenkins
How to Create a Perfect Home School by Lyle Lee Jenkins and Kelly Hawkinson Lippert

Perfect School Collection™ Resources

How to Create Math Experts series by Peggy McLean and Lyle Lee Jenkins
How to Create Math Experts with Fluency Quizzes by Peggy McLean and Lyle Lee Jenkins
How to Create Math Experts with Math Standards Quizzes by Peggy McLean, Laura Hayes and Lyle Lee Jenkins
How to Create a Math Foundation for Future Math Experts by Lyle Lee Jenkins
How to Create Bible Experts: Genesis to Revelation by Richard Douglas Junior Jenkins with Lyle Lee Jenkins

Early Readers

Bible Patterns for Young Readers series by Lyle Lee Jenkins
Aesop Patterns for Young Readers series by Lyle Lee Jenkins

Young Authors

Wordless Books for Young Authors series by Jim Chansler and Lyle Lee Jenkins

Special Project

All About Henry: Rich Widower of Savannah Valley by Lyle Lee Jenkins

CONTENTS

Introduction   1

Directions   3

Author's Purpose Booklet   5

Inference Booklet   7

Predictions Booklet   9

Evidence for Lessons Learned Booklet   11

Characters' Response to Challenges Booklet   13

Character's Perspectives Booklet   15

Another's Opinions/Claims Booklet   17

Literary Plots that are the Same and Different Booklet   19

Homophones Booklet   21

Bonus Booklets   23

Student Booklet Download   39

INTRODUCTION

The philosophy behind these booklets is that they are student-led, and elementary (K - 6) standards driven. In other words, students can independently complete much of the materials they are expected to learn in school with occasional pre-teaching.

The booklets are designed with a left-brain/right-brain balance. The back cover is a right-brain activity and the inside pages are clearly left-brain. The page prior to each grade level gives parents and teachers background knowledge and suggestions to successfully support their students and children through the booklets.

In order to create and assemble the booklets, parents and teachers can scan the QR code provided at the end of the book to download digital copies. To ensure proper printing, please utilize double sided printing and set your printer to "flip" on the short edge. The front page will be the front and back cover of the booklet. We have also included some bonus booklets within this series to support additional literary term exploration.

Enjoy,

Codi Hrouda, Emma McInerney and Lyle Lee Jenkins

GRADE 3
BOOKLET DIRECTIONS

My Second Book of Author's Purposes:
Students may need to be pre-taught on the ways authors write (persuade, inform, entertain, explain). Access to non-fiction/fiction examples of the author's purpose will be needed for this booklet.

My Book of Inferences:
Students will need to have access to fiction books.

My Next Book of Predictions:
Access to non-fiction books and coloring supplies will be needed for this booklet. Students may need review of text features and where to find them (table of contents, glossary, pictures and captions, graphs, and maps).

My Book of Evidence for Lessons Learned:
Students will need to have access to fiction books.

My Book of Character's Response to Challenges:
Students will need to have access to fiction books.

My Book of Character's Perspectives:
Students may need to be pre-taught perspectives and given examples. Access to a fiction book with more than one character's perspective and coloring supplies will be needed for this booklet.

My Book of Another's Opinions/Claims:
Students may need to be pre-taught opinions and claims. Access to a persuasive text will be needed for this booklet.

My Book of Literary Plots That are the Same and Different:
Students will need to have access to fiction books with similar plots with different cultural perspectives.

Some books we suggest:
Jumanji and *Zathura* both by Chris Van Allberg
Wemberly Worried and *Chrysanthemum* both by Kevin Henkes

My Book of Homophones:
Students may need to be pre-taught homophones.

Write to explain how to complete a certain task.
(example: build legos, make a recipe, draw something)

....

....

....

....

....

My Second Book of Author's Purpose

By: _____

School: _____

Teacher: _____

Date: _____

Authors write for different purposes. You have learned they write to persuade, inform, and entertain.
In addition to these, authors can also write to explain.

Explain - the author gives the reader direction on how to do something.
(Example: Recipe, user manual)

List titles of texts that are examples of the author's purpose of explain:

....

....

....

....

Match each author's purpose to it's correct example.
Some text examples could have more than one author's purpose.

A. Persuade   C. Inform

B. Entertain   D. Explain

Comic Strip _____   Commercial _____

Textbook _____   Instructions _____

Autobiography _____   Speech _____

Jokes _____   Poems _____

Student booklets are available via the QR code at the end of the book

Write a story with a problem and solution. Make sure to include enough details to help the reader make an inference as to how the problem will be solved.

_____

_____

_____

_____

_____

_____

_____

My Book of Inferences

By: _____

School: _____

Teacher: _____

Date: _____

An inference is to make an educated guess.
Read two books. First, identify the problem and then make an inference as to what the solution will be.
Then, write the actual solution. Give yourself a star if your inference was correct.

_____   _____
Title of Book 1   Title of Book 2

Problem: Problem:

_____   _____

_____   _____

Inference: Inference:

_____   _____

_____   _____

Continue Reading...   Continue Reading...
Solution: Solution:

_____   _____

_____   _____

Pretend you are writing a book about your favorite memory. Create a graph, map, and picture to help the reader make predictions about your book.

Graph: Map:

Picture(s):

Caption:

_____

My Next Book of Predictions

By: _____

School: _____

Teacher: _____

Date: _____

Using a non-fiction book, find the following text features and make a prediction of what the book will be about. Remember as you look at text features your predictions should become more detailed.

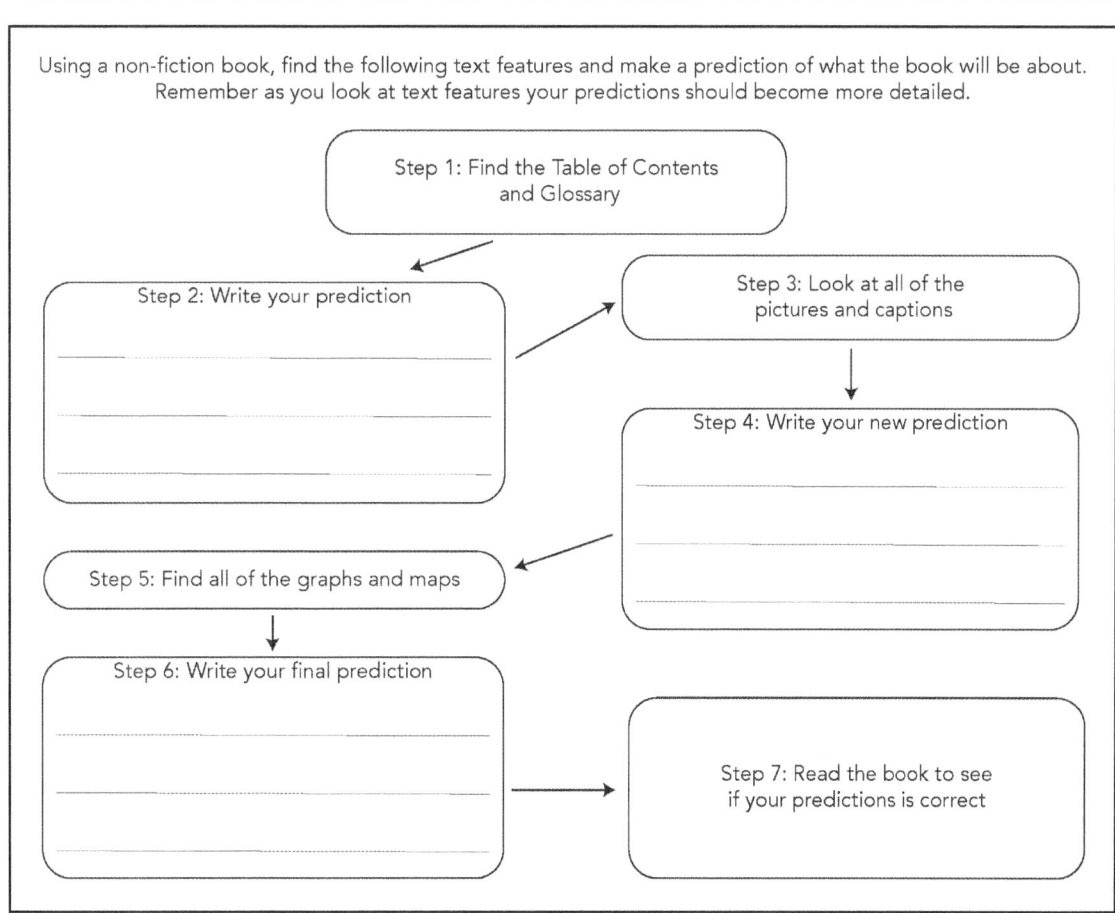

Step 1: Find the Table of Contents and Glossary

Step 2: Write your prediction

Step 3: Look at all of the pictures and captions

Step 4: Write your new prediction

Step 5: Find all of the graphs and maps

Step 6: Write your final prediction

Step 7: Read the book to see if your predictions is correct

Student booklets are available via the QR code at the end of the book

Describe a time you watched someone learn a life lesson.

_____

_____

_____

_____

_____

_____

_____

_____

My Book of Evidence for Lessons Learned

By: _____

School: _____

Teacher: _____

Date: _____

Read two fiction books and provide evidence that leads up to the lesson each character learns.

_____ | _____
Title of Book 1 | Title of Book 2

Evidence 1: | Evidence 1:

_____ | _____

_____ | _____

Evidence 2: | Evidence 2:

_____ | _____

_____ | _____

Lesson: | Lesson:

_____ | _____

_____ | _____

Student booklets are available via the QR code at the end of the book

Identify a time in your life when you were faced with a challenge. Describe how you responded to the challenge.

_____

_____

_____

_____

_____

_____

_____

My Book of Characters' Responses to Challenges

By: _____

School: _____

Teacher: _____

Date: _____

Read two fiction books and explain how the character in each book responded to the challenges they faced.

| _____ | _____ |
| Title of Book One | Title of Book Two |

Challenge 1:

_____

_____

Response 1:

_____

_____

Challenge 2:

_____

_____

Response 2:

_____

_____

Challenge 1:

_____

_____

Response 1:

_____

_____

Challenge 2:

_____

_____

Response 2:

_____

_____

Read a book with more than one character.
Draw a picture to show the two perspectives.

My Book of Character's Perspectives

By: _____

_____
Character's Name

School: _____

Teacher: _____

_____
Character's Name

Date: _____

Perspective - a character's attitude towards the world around them.

Read the short text and identify each character's perspective.

The Wildcats were on their way to the Championship basketball game. They rode the bus across town to face off their rivals, the Titans. In the bus, Katie was singing and dancing to the music hoping to make her teammates laugh. Annie sat quietly thinking, "I hope I don't make a mistake." As the bus screeched to a stop Annie wiped her sweating hands on her pants, while Katie yelled, "Let's go get 'em!"

Step 1: Underline evidence for Katie's perspective in blue.

Step 2: Underline evidence for Annie's perspective in red.

Step 3: Identify Katie's perspective
What is Katie's perspective?

_____
_____
_____

Step 4: Identify Annie's perspective
What is Annie's perspective?

_____
_____
_____

List your opinion on a certain topic.
Provide 2 claims to support your opinion.

Opinion:

_____

_____

_____

Supporting Claim:

_____

_____

_____

Supporting Claim:

_____

_____

_____

**My Book of Another's
Opinions/Claims**

By: _____

School: _____

Teacher: _____

Date: _____

Opinion - a personal view or judgment made about someone or something that isn't always based on facts.

Claim - The evidence the writer uses to prove their opinion. The claim can be tested to be proved true or false.

Mark each statement below as either an opinion or claim:

I hate peas.
◊ Opinion   ◊ Claim

Dogs make great pets.
◊ Opinion   ◊ Claim

Every other girl in the school has a cell phone.
◊ Opinion   ◊ Claim

Mystery books are better than science fiction books.
◊ Opinion   ◊ Claim

50 percent of Americans have visited Disney World.
◊ Opinion   ◊ Claim

Read a persuasive text and identify the author's opinion along with their claim.

_____
Title

Opinion:

_____

_____

_____

Claim:

_____

_____

_____

Student booklets are available via the QR code at the end of the book

Write a story that has a plot with both similarities and differences to a favorite book.

_____
_____
_____
_____
_____
_____
_____
_____
_____
_____

My Book of Literary Plots That are the Same and Different

By: _____

School: _____

Teacher: _____

Date: _____

Read two fiction books that are similar. Then identify similarities and differences in their plots (characters, setting, conflict, resolution, and lesson learned).

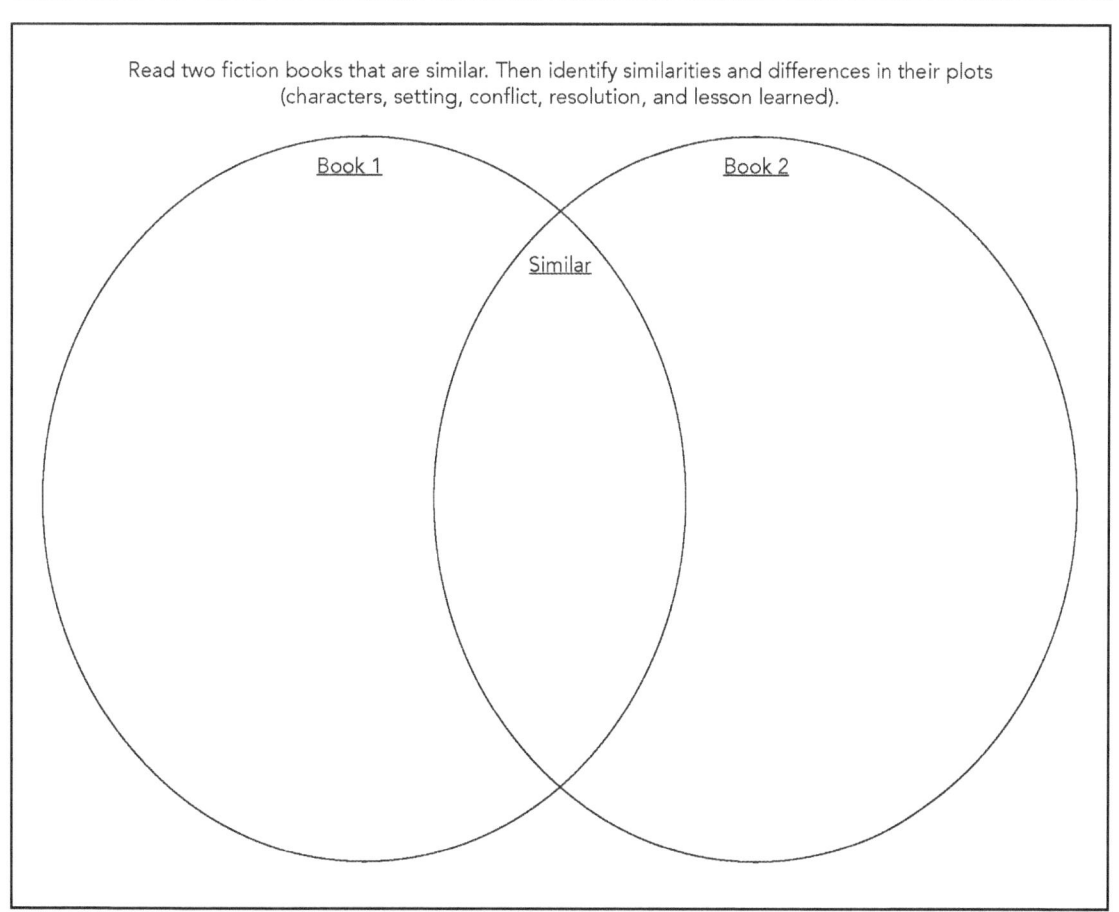

Book 1

Book 2

Similar

Write a homophone pair.
Draw a picture and write a sentence using both words.

My Book of Homophones

By: _____

| Homophone 1 | Homophone 2 |

School: _____

Teacher: _____

Date: _____

Homophones - words that sound the same, but have different meaning or spelling.
(example: hair and hare)

Match the homophone pairs:

Wait   Whole

Write   To

Hole   Bare

Two   Weight

Bear   Right

Underline the homophone that is used incorrectly in each sentence. Then rewrite the sentence using the correct homophone.

I stubbed my tow.

_____

The prince gave the princess a rows.

_____

Maria eight a hotdog at the game.

_____

My mom sent me to the store to bye apples.

_____

I nailed down the bored.

_____

CONTINUE CREATING LITERARY EXPERTS

BONUS BOOKLETS

A quick internet search for literary terms brings up hundreds of words. In addition, there are many topics to study as students gain more meaning from language and increase their writing skills.

Thus, the following blank pages are designed for students to write additional booklets about literary terms not included in *How to Create Language Experts with Literary Terms*. After selecting a new term, students select the format that best fits the task of writing about the literary term or concept.

There are times when children become so engrossed with a particular term that they want to make their booklet larger. These blank pages can also be used to add to existing booklets included in *How to Create Language Experts with Literary Terms*.

Student booklets are available via the QR code at the end of the book

My Book of _____

By: _____

School: _____

Teacher: _____

Date: _____

_____
Title of Book 1

_____
Title of Book 2

Student booklets are available via the QR code at the end of the book

My art:

Student booklets are available via the QR code at the end of the book

Book 1 Title: _____   Book 2 Title: _____

Book Title

Book Title

Student booklets are available via the QR code at the end of the book

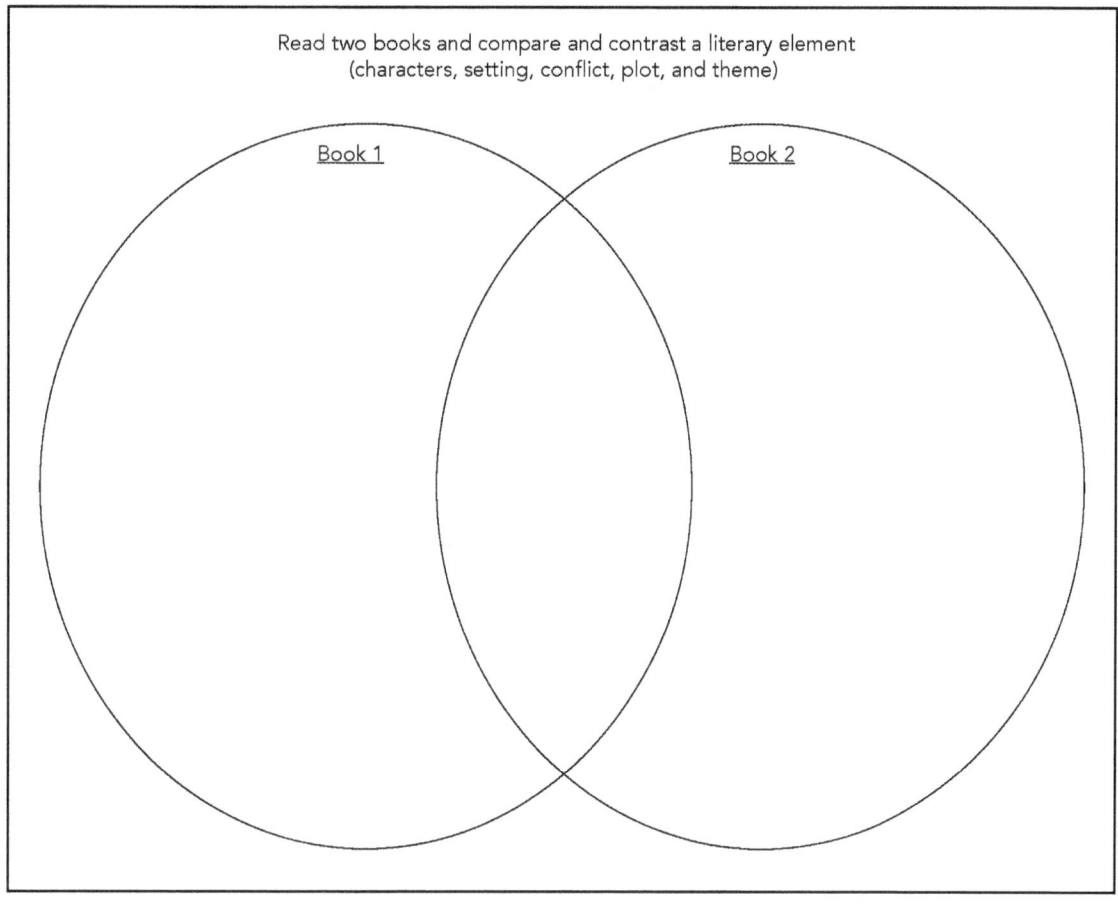

Read two books and compare and contrast a literary element
(characters, setting, conflict, plot, and theme)

Book 1

Book 2

Student booklets are available via the QR code at the end of the book

---

| Book Title | Book Title |

| Title of Book One | Title of Book Two |

Student booklets are available via the QR code at the end of the book

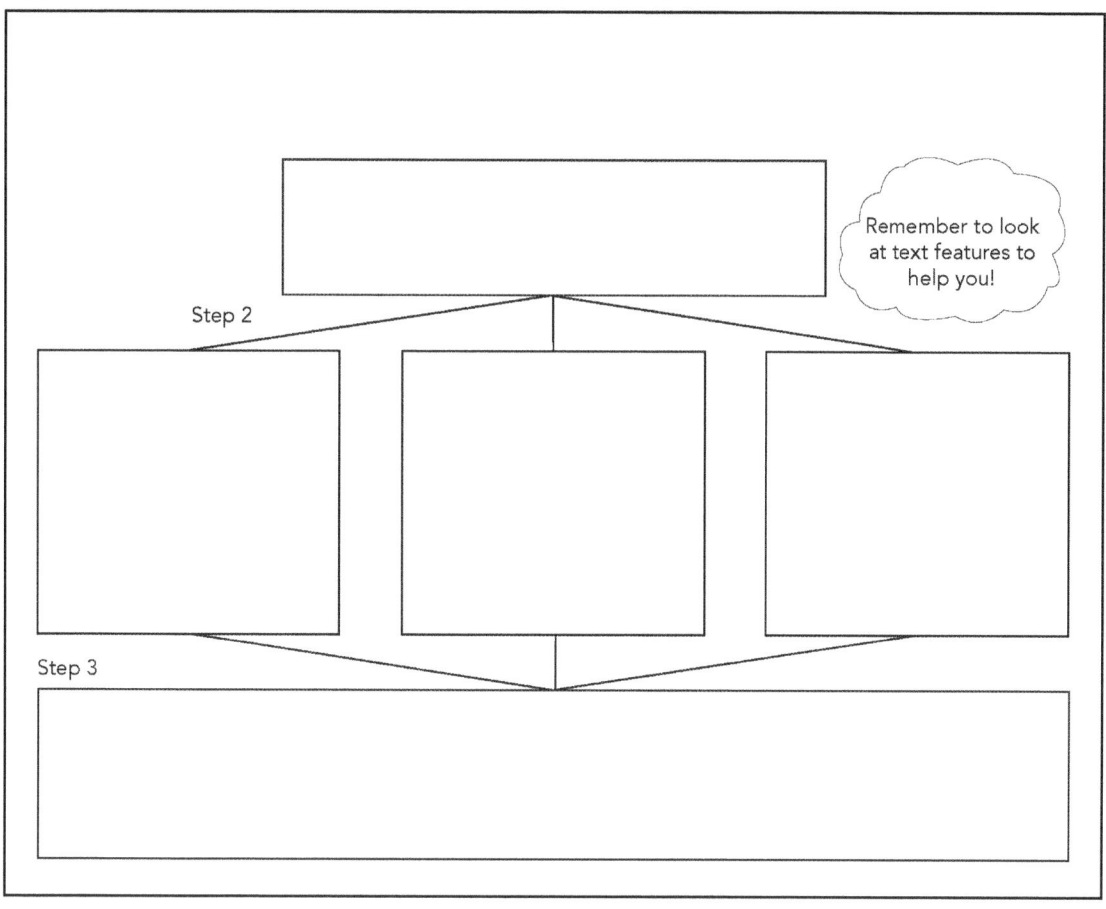

Remember to look at text features to help you!

Step 2

Step 3

Student booklets are available via the QR code at the end of the book

STUDENT BOOKLET DOWNLOAD

Purchasers of **How to Create Language Experts with Literary Terms** may use this QR code to download booklets from this book at no extra cost. This will ease the process of making copies for students and expand learning options. Both the print and digital download versions of this material are protected by copyright laws.

QR codes can be found in all LtoJ books, providing access to digital downloads of student worksheets.

ABOUT THE AUTHORS

Codi Hrouda grew up in the small town of Hubbard, Nebraska. After completing high school, Codi went on to pursue her degree in Elementary Education at Wayne State College, and graduated with a BA in Elementary Education in 2000.

Once graduated, Codi accepted her first job at Thurston Elementary School, in Thurston, Nebraska, as a fifth and sixth grade combination teacher. A year later, she and her husband moved to Columbus, Nebraska where she taught a year of first grade and then thirteen years of fourth grade at Centennial Elementary School. While teaching full-time in Columbus, she completed her master's degree in Curriculum and Instruction through Wayne State College. She graduated with her master's degree in May of 2006.

In 2014, Codi and her husband moved their family back to the area where she grew up to raise their three daughters. Codi accepted a fifth grade position at Dakota City Elementary in Dakota City, Nebraska where she continues to teach today. She just completed her twenty-second year of teaching in 2022. Codi spends her free time attending her daughters' activities, decorating, reading, and spending time with her family and friends.

Emma McInerney grew up in the small town of Elk Point, South Dakota. After completing high school, Emma went on to pursue a degree in healthcare at South Dakota State University (SDSU).

In 2015, she realized she was ready for a career change because her passion lies in education. She transferred to Dakota State University (DSU), earned a degree in Elementary Education, and graduated in 2019. Emma began her first job at Dakota City Elementary, in Dakota City, Nebraska, as a fifth grade teacher. While teaching full-time she completed her Masters degree in Curriculum and Instruction through Wayne State College, graduating in May of 2022. Emma concluded her third year of teaching in 2022, and she continues to teach alongside her co-author, Codi Hrouda.

Emma returned to her hometown of Elk Point after graduating, and spends her free time reading, gardening, and spending time with her boyfriend, family, and friends.

Dr. Lyle Lee Jenkins is an author, speaker, and recognized authority in improving educational outcomes. He believes that implementing a growth mindset and celebrating progress are the keys to helping students learn more and retain their enthusiasm for school.

His education experience, that spans over 50 years, ranges from working as a teacher, a principal, and a school superintendent in the California School System to being a University Professor. In 2003, Lyle Lee founded LtoJ, LLC hoping to impact and guide the way we approach education.

Lyle Lee Jenkins has authored six books showcasing continuous improvement in schools, including *How to Create a Perfect School*, *Optimize Your School*, *Permission to Forget*, *From Systems Thinking to Systemic Action*, *Improving Student Learning*, and *How to Create a Perfect Home School*. All literature offers powerful, practical suggestions for every aspect of education. The two most influential people supporting Dr. Jenkins's work are W. Edwards Deming and John Hattie.

Having spoken to educators all across the United States, Latin America, Europe, Australia, and Asia, Lyle Lee Jenkins is passionate about equipping the next generation with a true love of learning.

Dr. Lyle Lee Jenkins holds a Bachelor of Arts degree from Point Loma Nazarene University, a Masters of Education from San Jose State University and a Ph.D. from the Claremont Graduate University.

Lyle Lee Jenkins's website, www.LtoJ.net, is a great place to discover useful tools to guide your educational journey.

Do you have a great photo or video of your student using one of our products?

We would love the opportunity to share it on our website and social media channels!

Email us at info@ltoj.net

If you have a story to share, we would also like to hear from you. We feature student stories during presentations and on our social media accounts.

Our team loves sharing the joy of a child understanding new concepts. It allows our audience to experience firsthand the mission our team works towards every day; for students to maintain the same love of learning they brought to Kindergarten throughout all their years of schooling and into adulthood.

Thank you for being a loyal customer. We appreciate you!

The LtoJ Team

*Follow us on Instagram, Facebook, TikTok and YouTube
@LtoJLLC*

www.ingramcontent.com/pod-product-compliance
Lightning Source LLC
Chambersburg PA
CBHW081010120626
46546CB00010B/3090